The ◆ Lifesize
Animal Opposites Book

A DORLING KINDERSLEY BOOK

Note to Parents

The Lifesize Animal Opposites Book is an exciting introduction to the concept of opposites for you and your child to share. Read the lively rhymes that introduce each animal pair aloud and look together at the photographs. Encourage your child to identify the familiar animals, compare the differences and similarities between them, and then guess at the word opposites. In addition, your child will be using and learning new words as you talk about the animals, from the noises they make and what they look like, to just how big they really are.
Have fun with these lifesize animal opposites!

U.S. Assistant Editor Camela Decaire
Assistant Editor Fiona Campbell
Designer Ingrid Mason
Managing Editor Jane Yorke
Managing Art Editor Gillian Allan
Production Marguerite Fenn

Photography by Paul Bricknell, Jane Burton, Philip Dowell,
Michael Dunning, Steve Gorton, Frank Greenaway, Dave King,
Tim Ridley, Steve Shott, Kim Taylor, Barrie Watts, Jerry Young

First American Edition, 1994
2 4 6 8 10 9 7 5 3

Published in the United States by
Dorling Kindersley Publishing, Inc.,
95 Madison Avenue, New York, New York 10016

Library of Congress Cataloging–in–Publication Data

Davis, Lee [date]
   The Lifesize Animal Opposites Book / by Lee Davis.
      1st American ed.
         p.   cm.
   ISBN 1–56458–720–7
      1. Animals– –Miscellanea– –Juvenile literature.   [1. Animals–
   –Miscellanea.   2. English language– –Synonyms and antonyms.
   3. Questions and answers.]   I. Title.
QL49.D363   1994
591– –dc20   94–14988
                                                        CIP
                                                        AC

Color reproduction by Colourscan, Singapore
Printed and bound in Italy by L.E.G.O., Vicenza

The Lifesize
Animal Opposites Book
Lee Davis

DK

DORLING KINDERSLEY
LONDON • NEW YORK • STUTTGART

Back or front?

One cat is white,
the other is black,
The opposite of
front is back.

Which is which?

Long or short?

Toucan's beak is curved and long. Parakeet's beak is short and strong.

Which bird is flying?

Up or down?

Arctic fox stands
up to play.
Boxer dog lies
down all day.

Please get up, dog!

Hard or soft?

Hard or soft,
just how can you tell
A bushbaby's fur
from a tortoise's shell?

Touch and feel.

Big or little?

Little chicks, do you know
Just how big you will grow?

What fine feathers you're going to have!

13

Rough or smooth?

An egg is smooth.
What is rough?
Reptile skin is very tough.

Don't touch the crocodile!

Fast or slow?

Kittens can leap
and move so fast.
Snails are slow
and always last.

Hurry up, snails!

Open or shut?

Duck and ducklings,
side by side,
Whose bill is shut,
whose open wide?

Noisy or quiet?

Who wakes the house
with his noisy sound?
Who's quiet and quick
and scurries around?

"Cock-a-doodle-doo!"

Awake or asleep?

Wolf cub's awake,
touching a heap
That looks like fox cub,
fast asleep.

Sweet dreams, little fox.

Heavy or light?

Heavy baby elephant
holds his trunk up high.
Light little butterfly
flutters down nearby.

Hello, pretty butterfly!

"Whooo"
"Whooo"

Upside down
or right-side up?

Upside down, bat holds on tight.
Right-side up, owl sees at night.

In or out?

One hamster stays in,
the other goes out.
One is hungry,
but the other grows stout.

Come out and eat, little hamster!